Poets of Manor Mill

Monkton, MD

Copyright © 2024, Editors Robert R. Bowie Jr. and Mel Edden

Individual copyrights are held by the authors of the poems as noted herein.

All rights reserved.

ISBN 978-1-62806-412-4 (print | paperback)

Library of Congress Control Number 2024911441

Published by Salt Water Media
29 Broad Street, Suite 104
Berlin, MD 21811
www.saltwatermedia.com

Cover design by Paula Bogert
Cover photo by Bolling Willse Sr.
Illustration by Val Lucas, Bowerbox Press

Poets of Manor Mill

An anthology of poems written by featured poets and open mic participants

Volume I

Edited by
Robert R. Bowie Jr. and Mel Edden

FOREWORD

When I first met Angelo Otterbein, the proprietor of Manor Mill, and Cynthia Webber of the Hereford Branch of Baltimore County Public Library, in the fall of 2022 we talked about a collaboration to bring poetry to both locations. Shortly thereafter I met Mel Edden who had seen a flier at the library about our efforts. Mel had been given a notebook full of empty pages in which she had decided to write a poem a day for a year. This had launched her into an intensive exploration of writing and reading poetry.

From the beginning, Mel and I were in sync. Almost immediately, we suggested to Angelo and Cynthia that we should use this opportunity to nurture new and developing poets, and to support their development. The library offered us a workspace for teaching and discussion, and the Mill offered a welcoming and beautiful performance space. And so, our monthly poetry open mic nights at Manor Mill were born!

We held the open mics at the Mill on the first Monday night of each month so that new writers, often having attended the library workshop, could put their courage and their poems to the test. We had one rule: we would nurture and support participants, and any criticism was to be offered privately.

Angelo supported us, as he did all other types of artists and artisans who had been offered space and time to explore their passions at the Mill. The open mic nights were structured from the early days to begin with invited 'featured poets' who were published writers from the area, whether they be poetry professors from universities or locally-established, freelance poets. They were given fifteen minutes to open the program by reading a selection of their works, and by talking about their writing. After the first half an hour of these readings, we took a break so that the featured artists could sell their books and chat with participants of the open mic. Each open mic participant was then invited to read one poem and then, if time permitted, we went through the sign-up sheet again so each burgeoning poet had an opportunity to read a second poem.

From the beginning, this inviting and encouraging environment evolved into a growing community, born from mutual respect, conversation and performance. Over the last few years the growth has been remarkable, with a broad range of styles, technique and subject matter consistently represented. We look forward to enjoying this creativity and community for many more years to come.

The purpose of this publication is to celebrate the poetry community that has formed through our library workshops and open mic nights in Monkton. The poems contained in this first volume come from not only the participants of the open mics, but also from the featured poets who have headed up each month's program. Mel and I have selected one poem per person in order to show the quality and variety of poetry that has been shared at the Mill since we began. We have organised them to best represent our evolving poetry family at Manor Mill.

Mel and I would like to thank Paula Bogert, Susan Chase, Richard Edden, Tara A. Elliott, Stephanie L. Fowler, Matt Hohner and James P. Wagner for their assistance with this project. We also wish to give thanks to Bolling Willse Sr. for providing photographs and to Angelo Otterbein for his continued generosity and support of poetry at Manor Mill.

Congratulations to those who have been published! And, to the reader, we hope that these poems will entice you to come join us for a future open mic.

— Robert R. Bowie Jr.
September 2024

FEATURED POETS 2022 - 2023

Below is a list of our featured poets, from our very first open mic through to the end of 2023, most of whom have poetry featured in this volume.

November 2022	Select poets from the *Maryland Bards Poetry Review 2022*
December 2022	Dan Cuddy and Lauren H. Smith
February 2023	Jennifer Keith and Matt Hohner
March 2023	Alan C. Reese
April 2023	Michael Fallon and Jennifer A Sutherland
May 2023	Raymond Cummings, Thom Hawkins and Douglas Mowbray
June 2023	Winners of MPT Big Read Poetry Competition (Stephen Hollaway, Kathleen O'Toole and Douglas Mowbray)
July 2023	David Beaudouin and Alan Britt
August 2023	Kari Martindale and David Stant
September 2023	Shirley J. Brewer, Kathy Mangan and S.B. Merrow
October 2023	Stephen Hollaway and Steven Leyva
November 2023	Clarinda Harriss
December 2023	Susan Sonde

CONTENTS

Mark Brine • Manor Mill 1

Otis Sprow • Scandalous Kitchen 2

Shirley J. Brewer • Modern Torso of Apollo 3

Kathy Mangan • Husking Corn for Dinner, She Thinks of an Old Boyfriend 4

Steven Leyva • The Inner Habor's Octave 6

Matt Hohner • Driving at Night in the Rain, April 2021 7

Chrissy Stegman • A Pilgrim's Pace 8

Jennifer A Sutherland • Positioning 9

Alan Britt • Predator or Prey 10

Erika Miller • The Dictionary Habit 11

Virginia Crawford • Visiting the Formal Gardens 13

Clarinda Harriss • My Mother's Gifts 14

Michael Fallon • A Poem for My Father 15

David Stant • In Memory 16

S.B. Merrow • Genesis 17

Kari Martindale • Road Trippin' 18

Thom Hawkins • Autopsy 19

Douglas Mowbray • Point Person 20

Raymond Cummings • The Clouds Took Five 21

Heather Sowers • Beauty 22

Lauren H. Smith • Belonging 24

Ruhi Khanna • Tale of Butterfly 25

Rachel M. Novak • Safely on Shore 26

F. David Bolton • Sabotage 28

David Hofstetter • Nine Was Purple 29

Nicole Tsygan • the streets of new york 30

John Hutchinson • God's Work 32

Stephen Hollaway • Losing My Hearing on Block Island 33

Jennifer Keith • Rom Com 34

Jill Goodman • Doubt 36

Robert R. Bowie Jr. • Predawn Swim 37

Mel Edden • The Honey Pot 38

Matthew Milad Nikzad • A Stalemate 40

Alan C. Reese • In the Valley of Echoes 43

Bolling Willse Sr. • Advertising the Present 44

Zoe Leonard • House Spirit 45

Kaitlin Wachter • My Life is a Room 47

Derek H. Miller • Inside, A Fire 49

Dan Cuddy • Traveling To Grafenwöhr During A Military Exercise 50

Gary Siebert • War 52

Virginia Friedman • The Contentment of Trees 53

David Beaudouin • After Megan McShea 54

Biographies 57

Acknowledgments 69

The Poems

MANOR MILL

- *Mark Brine* -

Manor Mill.... just down the hill
where folks, they meet... to share their skill
of poetry... 'n arts & crafts...
conversations... jokes 'n laughs.

Painter's galleries... Old Time music...
Spring, summers, autumns... who couldn't use it?
Concerts, cook outs... creative times
to quell our wasteful, bored-filled minds.

Yes, Manor Mill... where they quilt 'n knit
in winter windows... with the candles lit,
beckoning warmth... camaraderie ... with a
homey-ness... tranquility.

Quaint 'n rustic... colonial look,
historic Monkton... a rural nook.
Yes, in these days... a getaway
from the mall-like mundane... mod. array.

So, come one, come all... to Manor Mill
— you're welcome here... ye, of goodwill!

SCANDALOUS KITCHEN

- Otis Sprow -

The kettle was flabbergasted
by the disparagements
from the pot.
The fork was outraged
by the short-cuts of the knife.
The knife was made livid
by the empty promises
of the fork.
While the spork
was a complete outcast
due to its mixed heritage.
And was anyone really surprised
when the dish ran away with the spoon?

MODERN TORSO OF APOLLO

- Shirley J. Brewer -

Sibley's Department Store boasted
intricate ceilings, ornate cash registers,
a pride of manufactured male bodies.
High school, I worked part-time
in men's underwear, pajamas, ties.

New stock arrived each week. My job:
undress the headless plastic gents,
reclothe them in the latest styles.
For bikini briefs, my boss made me
use the dreaded mini-mannequins.

Picture chest to upper leg—a shark
attack minus the gore. I would lean
backwards clutching my half-man,
remove his old undies, and with a swivel
or two, pull on the updated duds.

I became adept at handling torsos.
Romance came later. In the cool hours
before the store opened, when no one
was looking, I would grab a fiberglass
paramour, move like a dancer in heat

across polished floors—dreaming
of proms, chance encounters. Someday
soon I'd meet a guy with a face,
plus all his body parts. He'd talk back
to me, change his clothes daily,
take off his own underwear, then mine.

HUSKING CORN FOR DINNER, SHE THINKS OF AN OLD BOYFRIEND

- Kathy Mangan -

She tears back the green
blades – like so many rough
tongues – pinches the sticky
threads from crevices,
and lets the milky juices slick
her palms. They were nineteen,
freshmen, he was from Indiana
and worked summers de-tasseling
corn for DeKalb.

        It's dusk now
as she unzips the ears,
and she imagines him boarding
the flatbed at the company silos,
a yolk of July sun rising as they chug
out to counties called Vermillion,
Tippecanoe, Boone.

        Even now she sees
him arrive at the dew-drenched fields, male
and female rows stretching in a striped
half-mile, watches him bind
himself with bandanas and rubber-
tipped gloves, and –

       forty years gone –
her heart squeezes as she sees him roll down
his sleeves to button at his bony,
freckled wrists. She's now counting
the cobs as he wades into the wet
stalks. Steam rises and grasshoppers
leap at his thighs while he twists
and drops the first pollen-laden
tassels of the day.

       When she visited
from the East, they'd drive the back
roads of Brown County at night
in his mint green Rambler, then park and peel
each other – all fingers and knobs
and lips – in the gummy back seat, windows
rolled down to crickets and creaking
corn, his red hair brushing her cheeks
like shafts of strawberried light,
their teeth nibbling each other
as if they were biting into tight
kernels to burst the sugar.

THE INNER HABOR'S OCTAVE

- Steven Leyva -

    for C.

The only incorruptible sight here is the green of the camphor tree,
its rhizomes in your iris, extracting an oil. Scent on the wind raises

a Lazarus kiss we shared one harbor side afternoon, the algae
blooms hidden for once below the water's skin of sunlight.

The pig-iron colonial cannons all facing away. The horizon
unable to show any embarrassment, blushes hours after

we've left the hill, left it verdant and clinging to the gossip of cicadas.
Green is the color of cleaving. It has wrestled Eros from red.

DRIVING AT NIGHT IN THE RAIN, APRIL 2021

- *Matt Hohner* -

for Darryl, Rich, and Joél

Cool air like new breath through windows cracked
open just so, splatter of tires on wet asphalt, down
Cub Hill past the entrance to the Hickey Reform
School for Boys, past the Greek Orthodox church,
riding the brakes, then left at the bridge. A chorus
of spring peepers bubbles up from the Big Gunpowder
Falls, running high along its banks. New leaves soft
on the trees, filling in the dark spaces between amber
circles cast down from streetlights illuminating the road,
passing slower now than we ever took these bends
and hills—the dip-curve at Satyr Hill Road by the old
farm—how we fishtailed here at 90 m.p.h., careening
late to class one warm May morning our high school
senior year, the summer of our parting approaching
like truck headlights on high beam. How blind we were,
how confident. Now double guardrails glisten in the storm
where once only trees stood, trunks scarred by decades
of bad luck, drunken mishaps, a panicked swerve to miss
a doe. Down in the valley, old memories grip the shadows,
holding on for dear life. Rain streams across the windshield
like time, all those years wiped away, wiped away, wiped away.

A PILGRIM'S PACE

- Chrissy Stegman -

The day has found the
prayerful leaves and
walked her children of brightness
back from the night
and under her belly, in darkness grows;
a slow haze,
a spark that breaks,
up into the mouth of each leaf
and from its heart;
following a pilgrim's pace,
till the greenness
grows.
And every mouth is open upon the earth,
and none are left broken.
The day breaks the hand
of night in its hand, and says
forgive me, I can't look at you
and opens the bright face
of the flowers.

POSITIONING

- Jennifer A Sutherland -

The geese always know where to be,
and they arrive just in time. The reindeer

are never mistaken; invariably they shed
velvet, route the necessary blood and fat

to bone and hide. A caterpillar, at exactly
the right moment, begins to generate

the imaginal cells that will become wings,
antennae, once the novice body

has swallowed and digested itself. The fish,
when the coastline changes, trusts his prerogative

to swim. He goes where the current guides him.
I have been here, a long time, without deciding.

PREDATOR OR PREY

- Alan Britt -

    (After Federico García Lorca)

Insects seem to me far
more intelligent than we
give them credit for.

They lead lives so foreign
to our profane existence.

Imagine every day cultivating
traps of quicksand
for unsuspecting souls,
or adjusting the tension
on your web of faith?

Imagine living every single
hour of your life
as predator or prey?

Imagine if you're just a frilly
fish minding your business
below the blushing coral,
bothering no one,
before an arsenic lobster falls
upon your head and devours you?

Come to think of it,
humans and insects have more
in common than I thought.

So, does that make insects
more or less intelligent than
we give them credit for?

THE DICTIONARY HABIT

- Erika Miller -

A third grader, I receive The Webster College Dictionary
As a Christmas present from my parents
And the gift of advice: "Have the dictionary habit"
Which I do!
I also had a beloved pamphlet of word derivations
Typical was the story of King Tantalus in word and picture
The tree held down fruit it pulled back when reached for
So tantalizing to the king
So tantalizing to the third grader acquiring a taste for words
My friend and I went to Hershey Park with her family
Her dad was an school principal; her mother a teacher
Close to the park I suddenly point and say
"Look it's the ubiquitous Howard Johnson's"
Not said to impress; merely a fact
But I saw the parents look at each other and burst into laughter
They were intrigued
I was increasingly experiencing the power of words
The power of words
Taste them; they're succulent or bitter
Vital, humorous, stark, or litter
Do they bring clarity, and simplicity
Or possibly duplicity
Do they help coalesce a thought
Or are they cheap; have they been bought
The power of words
In a poem, story, or book
Makes you think; makes you look
Makes your mind resonate with others
Puts you in touch with sisters, brothers
You didn't even know you had
Connects you to the greatest thinkers

Helps you pull off those blinkers
Words-taste them, savor them
Flavor with them
Use them to love, cherish, and connect
The power of words

Disclosure: Thanks to the dictionary habit for making this poem possible.

VISITING THE FORMAL GARDENS

- *Virginia Crawford* -

my daughter runs away
with her partner and our dog. My son
slouches on a shaded bench with a novel.
Across the lawn, a woman in a golden gown
holds one hand at the base of her belly.
The photographer tilts the white reflective screen
to her best advantage. Between each pose
the father, in a crisp white shirt,
balloons the train so it drapes
perfectly down the stairs, fans across the lawn,
or swirls beside her. He remains
in several photos: standing behind her,
both their right hands under the belly
or peering into each other's
briefly perfect faces. They'll return to this moment
each time they see these photos in their dining room.
I marvel at the energy they've spent
to find the location, the gown,
to arrange her hair, apply her makeup,
pin the crown of flowers on her head.
Remembering how my husband fed me while
I nursed our babies, I know they don't have
much time. *Good luck with your
first baby,* I want to call.
*Enjoy yourselves
while you can. You'll never be this kind
of beautiful again. Practice saying goodbye.
Practice saying, "Everything will be okay,"
as if you believe it.*

MY MOTHER'S GIFTS

- Clarinda Harriss -

For my shapely mother, a shaped poem

My late mother and I shared a remarkable
   Talent for estimating exactly what
      Would fit into what. Our
        Parallel parking was
         Unparalleled.
        She would
         Glance
       At leftover soup
      And a leftover jar and
     Everyone would cry You can't fit
    This into that. "Funny," she'd say, neatly
   Pouring that into that, "I thought I could." She
Was one sarcastic bitch. It was among her best qualities.

A POEM FOR MY FATHER

- *Michael Fallon* -

It could only have been you
who lifted me to the high, thick branches
strong enough to hold my weight

the cherry tree all in bloom,
a white ship on a green sea
tacking north

and there among the murmur of bees' wings
I climbed through a cloud of blossom and

into the white heart of spring

IN MEMORY

- David Stant -

Morning comes.
Gray skies induce a seasonal sadness
Magnified by this winter's embrace of death.
A cold drizzle falls on my neck
sending chills down my spine
as I feel each drop.
I take shelter under the covered bridge
made of wood painted a faded red.
A lifetime of memories and regret exist here.

The sun appears and I begin my search.
The aquaduct, touched by the elements
but still standing in its entirety,
evokes thoughts of a man who had given so much
but whose significance aged out
of the lives of his children.
The light shines on this once grand structure,
Welcoming it if only for a moment back to its glory,
shadows spread along fields where men once sailed.

I see railroad tracks elevated
as they move past an old hardware store,
the stories he told me of his youth present in this moment.
My final words are said as his spirit boards the train,
white steam rising from the engine as he begins his journey
over the rivers, above the mountains, and into the abyss.
I see the sun's last light on this cold winter day,
offering its last comfort,
And I can only imagine I will see him again.

GENESIS

- S. B. Merrow -

From the beginning, then, with a wink of abandon—
like a trip downtown on an apple-red scooter,

a little crazy on the throttle, steering for the bumps and heaves,
for the joy when it leaps—the flawed engine of our freedom

has been *the word*—I mean, this is just, like, my opinion, man—
but the shout of yay or nay is our yes to play an elusive game,

to choose some fragrant fruit, dangerous and sweet, one of many
mysteries the biome sings today. They say it was woman,

then man, who dined and—right after god created the ocelot,
the unicorn, cilantro (which even then must have tasted

like soap)—brought us the choice to imagine, to *re-word*.
We head for the garden again and again, no longer ashamed

of our nakedness—hey, I'm just one red balloon winding
across a busy sky—and notice the many-gendered angels

arranging some kind of quartet. Listen to the tenor
of their voices, the occasional cymbal crash.

ROAD TRIPPIN'

- Kari Martindale -

Tallying roadkill, checking off license plates;
Will we ever spot Hawaii? Whizzing by signs
too fast to catch the letters—still looking for J.

Driving Day 4, somewhere around Wynebraskowa,
a red-tinted bingo window slides over my brain.

An unexpected Snake River waterfall
revives me; layers of puddles to slosh through,
my first time in the top of a waterfall—excited,
nervous, giddy, trying not to fall over, wishing
I was dressed for it.

Back on the road. Someone spies something blue.

AUTOPSY

- Thom Hawkins -

I accidentally set my bills to 'autopsy',
a simple typo, but the bankers followed
through, in their silk ties and white coats,
prodding at my statements with ballpoint,
looking for the cause of default.

POINT PERSON

- Douglas Mowbray -

At some point,
you may make a point;
you may have a point;
you may be on point;
you may make an appointment;
you may have an appointment;
you may be appointed.

At some point,
you will be the point;
you will be the appointment;
you will be the appointed.

At all points,
you are the point;
you are the appointment;
you are the appointed.

THE CLOUDS TOOK FIVE

- *Raymond Cummings* -

If magic hour was late to set, the crew
weren't sweating it. Production assistants
don't alienate themselves and a stylist daubs
the singer's face alabaster and tempestuous

smoke machines threaten to slide into the
ocean and the cinematographer perches
on a Marshall stack situated on a stage
atop a cliff looking out over the Pacific,

lighting a joint. Extras laze, or graze.
The hirsute keyboard player dons a lei
and an unbuttoned shirt the color of
Massachusetts. A *Rolling Stone* stringer

solicits quotes from the director, and
yet: what's to say? It's the third single
from the fourth LP and no one will see
this video. But the drummer's sleeves

are rolled up now and the guitarist strums
"Eight Days A Week" for some trembling
Make-A-Wish kid and Tiki torches burn
black. As the horizon slowly turns intense

and improbable the director feels the breath
catch in his chest and then he nods up at the
cinematographer who eases down, nods back.

At the snap of her fingers, the clouds take five.

BEAUTY

- Heather Sowers -

And a dreamer said, speak to us of Beauty.
And she answered –

Do not look for her on TV screens and fashion runways
or splashed across a new hit CD
She dwells in the longest line at Wal-Mart
standing on feet swollen from working all day
Do not seek her in triple X movies or cheap thrills
for she has a wildness that comes
from the hot core of the Earth
up through her bare feet, thick calves and silky thighs
It explodes from within her, a brazen fire
that turns silicon and collagen into pathetic piles of putty

The bored and the lazy say –
We have found her in the lines of this plastic pop song

And I say, Nay!
Beauty glows in the eyes of the old man
doing the dishes by the light of one cheap bulb,
flows from the voice of a woman who sings true
Beauty breathes with the husband
who sobs at his wife's grave
She lives in the hands of a woman who
scrubs floors and toilets in order to feed her family

You cannot cage Beauty, bottle it up
and sell it in the cosmetics aisle
You cannot package it
with a dozen pesticide laden flowers
and claim you have found it

Beauty shines in the smile of a father
dancing in the yard with his children
She sparkles in the laughter of a girl
jumping barefoot in a mud puddle
I trace the map of her journey
in the lines on my grandmother's face

Beauty pulses in the heart of the tamarack,
flows through the blood of the raven and dove
She is the lupine that grows
on the mountainside in the early sweetness of spring
She stands amongst juniper and moonshadows,
outlined black against the midnight-blue sky
Beauty caresses those full of pain or sorrow
like raindrops on a rose
She burns through fear and doubt
with the strength of a thousand suns,
leaving only grace in her wake
The thoughtful and the brave say –
We have seen her in the silent starry sky
streaking through the heavens
The pure and the loving say –
We feel her arms wrap 'round us
in the snowy depths of winter

Beauty is not free –
her price is sweat and the salt of countless tears
Beauty is the seed and the sower,
the root and the bloom
She fills the silence
between the words of this poem

BELONGING

- Lauren H. Smith -

You are more than a body.
Your body is you.
Don't beat it into submission
with food deprivation and exercise
with busyness and work
and overwork
and overwork
(why overwork?)

Don't talk to your body the way
your mother talks to hers
when she pinches at her belly and shields her face
from her own photograph
Don't talk to it the way she talked to yours
when you were growing up,
already insecure enough

Do you wear the disdain she bears?
You don't have to.
You can pull on your own clothes.
You can write your narrative about the precious flesh housing your heart,
holding sensations like velvet imprints—
memories and trauma, strength and
stories stored in its folds

You belong in your own skin,
your own damn beautiful skin,
the pages of powerful you.

TALE OF BUTTERFLY

- Ruhi Khanna -

Winter lights make way for longer days
The roses perk up,
Lawns turn green,
Young leaves invite deer,
Gloves change reasons,
Blossom gives hope,
Robin's song wakes the world,
Lost colors return,
The love calls the rains,
Caterpillar feast turns into greed
Metamorphosis is happening
As the world waits for new beginning,
Let's share the change,
And all go through the metamorphosis,
And emerge to make the world
As beautiful as a butterfly.

SAFELY ON SHORE

- Rachel M. Novak -

Do you dare to enter into a world,
so complex as "the girl"?
The view from the shore may tempt your folly,
but you must be accepting of the whole, and by golly...
The ocean is where uncharted challenges may arise,
with her churning waters and turning tides.
Ahhh but also where the real beauty begins...
where the creator placed His mark
— claiming her all of her sins.
Where questions beg for answers
and ideas are birthed...
of course you could stay on the shore
grasping to the comfort of the earth.
Selfish you'd be — a fool if I dare.
How unfair, to the maiden
that is told to stay small.
That's not what He made her
for that's not it at all.
Not meant as a trophy
to be won for your arm,
for if that's all you allow,
you'll cause irreparable harm.
For a time, satisfactory
but then surely all will crumble.
There's a difference you see
between being "muted",
and being humble.
She's a worthy adversary
— a "winged soldier" if you will.

For there are battles happening just over every hill.
Trust in the magic and trust in the heart,
for you'll never really know her
if you ignore the depths from the start.
He's instilled bravery, determination and grit,
along with a sense of wonder
and a pretty quick wit.
You see, everything you're lacking,
and for everything you crave,
you must endure the crashing of a few little waves.
Perhaps the seas could be calmed
with a peaceful and understanding mind.
What if at the bottom, along with the wreckage,
it would be a real treasure that you'd find?
I suppose you'll never really know
if you stay safely on the shore...
but as for the girl,
like the sea she'll keep raging.
You see, she's worthy of so much more.

SABOTAGE

- F. David Bolton -

I'm at war with inanimate objects.
They started it.
Packages choking in plastic.
Zip locks. Tear here. Where's here?
The unopened jar of peanut butter mocking fingers
The neck of a bourbon bottle wrapped in black plastic
The 25-foot hose attached to pipe
refusing to budge this winter's eve
Keys that stick, vapes that clog, tires that leak
Child seats requiring an engineer to connect
Umbrellas open only to the sun
It's enough to make me numb to Trump
Gotta concentrate on what's at hand
Lest I forget reading glasses, marking places
     living room, bedroom, office and kitchen.
Insidious how they move about
Once found all six
blending into a mahogany stand
Gotcha! Way to go, old man.

NINE WAS PURPLE

- David Hofstetter -

I'm keeping track of colors these days
Like a trainspotter, recording every pass-through
Reds and blues, all the easy ones, but what about
that green in the sky right before a tornado?
What the hell is that?
It's green and not green and what's it doing in the sky?
Or the yellow my urine was this morning
It's not Chinese Imperial Yellow
Or any other yellow of my life and I don't like it
In school I knew a girl who instantly calculated
the number of syllables in any sentence spoken to her
And divided by three
She didn't know why she did it
Embarrassed by her obsession but proud of her skill
And each quotient had a color
Nine was purple, I remember
She seemed normal
That's a good one - normal
I'll have to remember that

THE STREETS OF NEW YORK

- Nicole Tsygan -

i stand in the streets of new york
pouring rain, a herd of us high schoolers
that just got off the bus
flocks of umbrellas forging our way through
to central park
and broadway

i stand in the streets of central park
dripping with rain and smiles
'look!
a bleeding heart!
a canada goose!
a pigeon!'
we listen to facts from our teacher
and splash through puddles
picking our way over cobbles and asphalt

i stand in the streets of new york
just outside the streets of central park
my jacket fully soaked through
stealing a bite of overpriced pretzel
entertaining my friend by
saying song lyrics
in an impression of a russian slam poet
we laugh on this sidewalk, toes against the sewer grate

i stand in the streets of new york
having walked a mile to wait in line for broadway
during which a pigeon launched itself directly at my head
my friend laughed out
'is that enough pigeon for you?'

i replied
'haha! never!'
as we pressed together
under the ceiling of umbrellas

i stand in the lobby with my ticket
stand in the queue to get paper towels
stand at my seat
sit in my seat
am glued to my seat
when the show starts
i am riveted

i stand again on the streets of new york
dripping rain and speechless praise

i sit in a bus on the streets of new york
drenched beyond measure
pulling off waterlogged layers of jackets
freeing myself from wet socks and wetter shoes
when my teacher yells
'so how'd you guys like the show'
and we all scream, cheer, yell back
'oh my god it was incredible'

i stand on the street outside my school
still damp
still thinking about the show
waiting for my dad to pick us up
and i think
'wow'
'what a gloriously wonderful day in new york'

GOD'S WORK

- John Hutchinson -

The February *Sports Illustrated* swimsuit
issue arrived. You know,
the one they say American males
warm for
in a cold month.

I looked, flipped through the pages,
thought, *So what? It's just*
another woman,
another attractive woman in a bikini
with much exposed skin and

little left for the imagination.
Then wondered, *What's my problem,*
is it just an off day or maybe
age eighty-two, God's planned
obsolescence at work?

LOSING MY HEARING ON BLOCK ISLAND

- Stephen Hollaway -

for my wife

Even in my dreams I cannot make out what you say
over the chronic crickets, high time's whine,

over the roar and suck of the tide outside my window,
God's incessant wind hushing the rub of tires on tar.

The flags slap themselves awake, gulls flap and call,
few humans listen to white noise in deep March.

Behind it all you are speaking, and I am reading your lips,
your eyes are urging me to listen to the words.

You are the light on the end of my island signaling
in a fog in a code I must once have known.

You looking at me through the Fresnel lens
can see how sound comes through chopped and stacked.

If you understand this, speak into my hand like water,
flow over the worn stones of my beach until I hear.

ROM COM

- Jennifer Keith -

You reach a certain age when you know
the difference between a play bark and a warning bark
even when you don't have dogs.

At about this same time, you realize why
you've always hated the films about adorable people
and a universe that yearns

to promote them to the nuptial industrial complex
of sudden, final happy endings that have nothing and everything
to do with strip center glass massageries.

If you watch one more young woman puff
her hair out of her eyes with exasperation,
you will become an arsonist with extreme prejudice,

torching the little bakery, the precious bookstore,
the darling cafe, the sweet, white gazebo
and snow-frosted holiday inn

but leaving this stand, untouched: a tiny diner
with grease-lacquered walls where the cook
leans over his partition with tragic eyes

and informs me the waffle iron has a short
and he cannot make it work. By this time,
alternatives are fine — I say yes to pancakes

and yes to the chance of forgiveness
that I begged you to ask for and you did
and I said yes, your words in a box of robin's egg blue.

Bring up the music in the soundtrack, whether incidental
or Gladys Knight — neither one of us will remember
and neither, thank the stars, will sing along

with battered spoons held up like microphones.
We have weirder fish and grits to fry.
Delivered on those thick, dishwasher-hot platters

is a rolling-out red carpet of make-up nonsex, nonsense
with fate giving the laces of our sneakers a reassuring yank
and tying the bow loops in an overhand for safety.

And we will run, a car packed with pink and blue suitcases,
a plaid Thermos and a drowsy leopard,
blowing a pop stand of personal grievance.

The whole diner is applauding now, with me wanting
the whole of this tear-stained and bloody, badly written world
to have what I'm having.

DOUBT

- Jill Goodman -

The green hue developed slowly.
It's been green for a week.

I asked him if the water seemed green.
No, he said, it's just a refraction of light.

It tastes ok,
but, it's not right.

After he left,
I took the pitcher apart.

I washed the filter,
the spout,
all of it,
inside and out.

Now the water is clear,
colorless.
Why do I filter myself through him?

PREDAWN SWIM

- Robert R. Bowie Jr. -

The fireflies burn out well beneath the stars
And leave the shadows of the trees around me,
Naked here, in a galaxy of war.
Poolside, in my moon reflection, I will be

Dropping out of this humid world down to
The unexpected. Guillotined to cold;
Feet first with the water closing over you
And then shoving off the pool bottom, old

And stretching out as the new world runs by
Drifting utterly empty, my life gone
In my underwater wake and my eyes
Closed till I hit the wall and stand alone

In the shallow end, and I am reborn,
Baptized I rise, with the coming of the morn.

THE HONEY POT

- *Mel Edden* -

sits on the most easy to reach shelf
of our walk-in kitchen pantry.
It is not one of those earthy

stoneware pots, glazed in sandy
brown that you would find
in the paws of Winnie the Pooh.

Instead, it is Rubbermaid circa 2015,
solid, square-prismed with rounded
corners, a red lid that tightly fits.

Purchased, initially, with one
purpose in mind: to hide from the ants
our honey, syrup, Nutella etc,

over the years, it has evolved
to hold a deeper purpose —
one I now attempt to put into words:

Sore throats are soothed with lemon
and ginger. *Fetch me the honey pot*
I say, gently, as the kettle boils.

Porridge on cold days before school
is a winter treat. *Shall we add honey?*
Hopeful heads nod and anticipate.

The outrageous 5:30 alarm vibrates
awaking a zombie teen. Sympathetically,
I swirl honey in chai for the long bus ride.

Lazy Sundays, just the four of us, means —
pancakes in pajamas! The honey pot
provides something delicious to drizzle.

You see? There is ritual to reaching
for that plastic honey pot
and its contents smooth and sweet.

It is comfort. It is family. It is love.

A STALEMATE

- *Matthew Milad Nikzad* -

Let me tell you a story about Iran
in the '80s: when ladies put their hijabs on
and Khorramshahr was invaded by Saddam
who dropped mustard gas on my own dad and mom
He bombed throughout Iran like a maniac
while the West fought against us and helped Iraq.
For eight whole years, we held up our backs,
and they wonder why we hate to see the Union Jack.

Here's the flashback: 1980
Iran is out with the Shah and in with Khomeini.
Then, amidst the chaos and the lack of order,
Iraqi tanks start coming across the border
and start firing, the liberation army is hiring,
Mohammad Hossein Fahmideh is so inspiring,
he halted the advance of a whole brigade
with his tiny body overtop a hand grenade.

So began the conflict—no ceasefire.
Prisoners of War held behind barbed wire.
Saddam's soldiers thinking so nationally
that they forgot to think rationally, using
chemical weapons on Iranian civilians,
civilian casualties approximately millions,
and everyone knew Iraq was violent,
and yet the world decided to stay silent.

Bombs in Ahvaz, night sky turning red
More tanks arrived as thousands fled
I know it might be hard to relate to me,
just picture your own mom as a refugee.
She lost everything—childhood home turned to ashes
They ran away when they saw the red flashes
Forget the gold, rugs, or scriptures,
My mom misses her baby pictures.

But tables turn, undeniable victory!
Khorammshahr liberated, war's almost history,
but no, Iran wanted more soldiers on their end
That's when my dad lost his two best friends—
A terrible loss or just another statistic?
Missiles ballistic, war hawks militaristic
My dad sent his friends a Christmas card
but the post office doesn't deliver to graveyards.

1982, it's Iran on the offensive
'83, the war's getting expensive
'84, tactics getting more complex
'85, we start to feel the war's effects
'86, then starts politics' awareness
'87, Iran's feeling war weariness
'88, we need to end this war quickly,
there are holy sites in these cities.

So many countries try Iran, it's funny
They always have an eye on our oil money.
I'm here at the graves of my dad's best friends
and Ahmad's tombstone is where my story ends.

In short, nothing but mourning for the martyrs,
For a war caused by Saddam and his partners
We hoped that the war would've been shortened,
But the world didn't give their support and
damaged a country's society.
Countless losses, but we grieved silently.
My mom is still hurting, the war's still within her,
and the worst part about it was—
there was no winner.

a stalemate

IN THE VALLEY OF ECHOES

- Alan C. Reese -

While there are an estimated 7,000 languages spoken around the world today, one of them dies out about every two weeks... – Associated Press

Listen—

the vibrations of our voices
weaken with each passing hour
and soon we will intone no more.

Can you bear to witness
centuries evaporate
and all that we contain of

time and seasons,
sea creatures and reindeer,
landscape and myth,

math and music,
the commonplace
and the unknown

encased in syllable and sound
dry up and blow away
across the horizon

of your own wonder?

ADVERTISING THE PRESENT

- Bolling Willse Sr. -

Which came first:
The tick or the clock?
The heartbeat or the hunger?
The sound or the silence?
Our inner-clock or the church bell?

Who sets our inner-clock? Is it
Our world spinning – our circadian rhythms,
our loved ones, or our job?
Is Time on our side,
Or is it our nemesis?

The world spins counterclockwise!
It spins slower at its poles
than at the equator.

Time is not a problem,
It is our mis-understanding
of time's relativity.

Reset your inner clock!
Set it for the Present (for me that is 10:10).
Stop worrying about your time line,
Concentrate on how wide it is!
Make Time, don't Be Timed.
Give Time... Kindness is the birthplace of Hope.
A stopped clock is right twice a day
and that is good enough for NOW!

HOUSE SPIRIT

- Zoe Leonard -

the spirit of a house (or building), strengthened by the energy of those caring for it. When the spirit of a house is very strong, it may begin to manifest physically. My particular house spirit communicated to us through a blinking light in the living room.

We brought her out of the walls,
out of the foundation.
Our love made this house alive,
and I am in love with her.

I spend hours in the living room
staring at the light.
Her heart beats like mine.
I want to be like her, wholly.

I burn incense,
I play music she likes, and dance
(she dances) to music we all like.
I build the altar, and breathe in.

I spend hours in the living room,
even longer in the kitchen
cooking a meal for six, the seventh
chatters down the hall.

Yes, I see you,
my dear, are you
talking? What do you want
except for us
to be happy

expect for dinner to be home made
and us sitting around the table,
except for flowers in a vase,
a wreath hanging from the door,
for drinks to be poured,
for guests on the couch, served
a piece of what we made ourselves,

for the light to flood in,
for me to vacuum the floors,
for the plants to be watered,
for the kettle to steam in the morning.

For me to dream of her
when I'm gone.

// *after*

I land back in Maryland (*will I see you again?*) I can hardly see the road in front of me (*will you vacuum every week?*) and what's here has always been here (*cook dinner every once in a while, remember?*) until I stumble into a place (*will I be there?*) and from the lights strung above me (*the light is blinking*) a light is blinking.

Can I build my heart again, with you?

MY LIFE IS A ROOM

- Kaitlin Wachter -

My life is a room
As a child it was small
It fit me and my childish thoughts
Then I grew

As I met new people
And learned new things
The room expanded
As people left, holes were left
Doorways they passed through
Letting others come in
But the room never shrunk

Someone took a hammer
Built an addition on my life
For them to occupy
Just a corner
A while later they left
The space lay vacant
The empty yawning space
Threatening to swallow me
Drown me in darkness

So I started to fill the corner
Patched the doorway
Bricked the window
Until the corner lay in darkness
Stuffy dusty littered with
Music and memories and moments
Loved, treasured but unseen
Until I roused myself

Pulled out of a haze of grief
And confronted the darkness
The hammer lay where it was left
I took it up and with my own hands
Opened the window, opened the door
I let in light, dusted the frames
Threw to the curb
The music the memories the moments
I had no more use for

And in this corner - my own room
I finally claimed, finally cleared
A little space for me

INSIDE, A FIRE

- Derek H. Miller -

Beside
there is a calm fire,
mostly embers, really.
Suffuse coals, orange-red, cracked ash—
pulsing potential to set this small world aglow.

A place to warm
over-worked hands
and tired feet.
Space to gather,
to share, to laugh—
lingering in silent warmth,
shedding light
on the small circle
holding us knee-to-knee.

Embers which, fatedly, (re)turn to ash.

Inside,
there is a calm fire,
without being stirred,
without kindling to feed,
overly-shielded and smothered from Wind.
the inside, burns out.

Keep the Flame.
Poke. Prod. Stoke. Stir.
Tend. Shift. Move.
Breathe…blow so gently, so steadily.
Burn strong, hot, wild.
But not outside
Burn in—
But not out.

TRAVELING TO GRAFENWÖHR DURING A MILITARY EXERCISE

- Dan Cuddy -

The convoy strains uphill,
observing the double white lines
civilians paint for tentative order
when night erodes all but the headlights.
The rational stabs of light poke at the road
But their thrust is only forward.

In the back of the trucks
empty watercans clank with the bumps;
helmets, thoughts, rifle butts are jostled, jolted
by machines built for war, not comfort.

Tired, cold, holding on
to stop from sliding on the wooden bench,
I look out from that womb of canvas,
look out at the forest and its darkness,
created by the truck headlights following behind.

Through Old World villages we pass,
one by one, nameless from this view,
this backward glancing.

I remember after leaving,
the smell of horse dung, mold,
the dark alligator-skin gray stone,
the black blank windows,
my imagining the lives asleep
in those medieval peasant buildings
huddled against the night air,
like a stopped wagon train.

I picture a farmgirl,
her face taken from a Vogue cover,
sleeping beneath a warm quilt,
the swell of her breasts, her dawn-like hair
spreading its rays out on the pillow
as if painted by Botticelli.

This picturing does nothing
but harden me in frustration,
and there is no release from the facts,
a snake of trucks
winding through my enchanted landscape
like a soldier's four-letter words.

WAR

- Gary Siebert -

"Bombs bursting in air"
I am an heir
to bombs bursting on the ground
where I have found
still to be alive
where thousands died.

Bullets left
bullets right,
My best friend died
in a hail of fire,
but the desire
is to live
beyond this carnage
of human flesh and blood.

Irony is not lost on God
to whom
both sides pray
for victory.
Is not the devil
stirring the pot?
But not
The Almighty Architect of the Universe?

Does a person's ego
surpass the welfare of a nation?
Of a tribe, a clan
a family of people
intertwined by common roots?
Does Mother Nature
play a role
to cull the herd
with conflict and conflagration?

THE CONTENTMENT OF TREES

- Virginia Friedman -

No matter the season
Trees stand strong and confident
No difference it makes
From the glorious days of spring
When new clothes are being stitched
To the lush and extravagant designs of summer
The delightful hues of fall
Don't puff up their egos
And even in winter
When their clothes disappear
And they stand there
Exposed
Stark naked
They're comfortable in their own bark.
Never mind the gnarly knots
Or the fungus readily seen
They know who they are
And why they're on this earth
To comments made by others
They pay no heed
They have nothing to hide
No need for fig leaves
They're comfortable in their own bark.

AFTER MEGAN MCSHEA

- David Beaudouin -

Don't ask me - I don't know. A sudden light
then the sleeping city rises to meet
me, whole as if in some dumb dream, I rise
too and slipping on your jacket, run to
catch the ferry from that place of the living,
sort of. A car horn "honks," mysteriously.
Then a coffee, archipelago of faces
rush forward and back, adrift my throbbing
brain desires only for questions to
devour the answers. I'm that tough, like
you. Baffle and waffle cling to each other,
longing that rhyme. This is an old way of
talking or of being. Enormities
will follow thus. All love lies in the seeing.

BIOGRAPHIES

David Beaudouin, Baltimorean, is a widely published poet and performer. He was the founder of Tropos Press (1976-2001), one of the region's earliest and most respected alternative literary presses, as well as the literary magazine *The Pearl* (1980-2001). Published works include *Ten Poems* (1973), *Gig* (1976), *Catenae* (1989), *Ode to Stella* (1990), *American Night* (1992), and *Human Nature* (1995). Two new collections, *After All* (Bowerbox Press) and *Some Odes and Others* (UnCollected Press) will be published in 2024.

F. David Bolton. After decades in advertising and PR, taught professional writing for twelve years at the University of Maryland. He left in 2015 so he could devote himself to fiction. Out of that came a pre-Columbian fable, *Love Thief: The Legend of Ixmal the Healer*. Kirkus Reviews cited it as one of the best books in 2019, "an excellent tale that serves as both a thriller and anthropological portrait." Next came a poetry book, *A Mind Full of Nothing*, (poetscoop.org/free.htm#MFON_DAVIDB) and another novel, *Love is where you find it*, now in quest of a publisher.

Robert R. Bowie Jr. is a poet and playwright who has had plays performed in Baltimore and New York. He is the Harvard Alumni Association's poet, laureate. His poems from his book *An Accidental Diary*, (for sale on Amazon), have been anthologized and awarded first runner up for the Robert Frost Poetry prize 2022. His blog posts can be found on his website Robertbowiejr.com, Facebook, Instagram, Twitter and LinkedIn. He lives with his wife in Monkton.

Shirley J. Brewer (Baltimore, MD) serves as poet-in-residence at Carver Center for the Arts. Her poems garnish *Barrow Street, Passager, Gargoyle, Poetry East, Loch Raven Review*, among other journals and anthologies. Shirley's poetry books include *A Little Breast Music* (Passager Books), *After Words* (Apprentice House Press), *Bistro in Another Realm* (Main Street Rag), and *Wild Girls* (Apprentice House Press). Interviewed in January, 2020 by Maryland poet laureate, Grace Cavalieri, for her series "The Poet and the Poem" at the Library of Congress, Shirley's poems are part of the Lunar Codex program, and are currently on the moon! shirleyjbrewer.com

Mark Brine is a folk-country-blues musician/songwriter, a published author (two adult-level novels, three children's) and has had numerous poems published throughout the years. He presently resides in Baldwin, MD and is active in all the noted. www.markbrine.com

Alan Britt has been nominated for the 2021 International Janus Pannonius Prize awarded by the Hungarian Centre of PEN International for excellence in poetry from any part of the world. Previous nominated recipients include Lawrence Ferlinghetti, Charles Bernstein and Yves Bonnefoy. He has published twenty-five books of poetry and was interviewed at The Library of Congress for *The Poet and the Poem*. A graduate of the Writing Seminars at Johns Hopkins University he currently teaches English/Creative Writing at Towson University.

Virginia Crawford has been a long-time teaching artist with the Maryland State Arts Council. She earned her BFA from Emerson College, Boston, and her Master of Letters from the University of St. Andrews, Scotland. Her books are *Touch* from Finishing Line Press and *questions for water* from Apprentice House Press. She currently teaches English Language Development at the elementary level with Baltimore County Public Schools.

Dan Cuddy is currently an editor of the *Loch Raven Review*. In the past he was a contributing editor of the *Maryland Poetry Review* and *Lite: Baltimore's Literary Newspaper*. He has had a book of poetry published "Handprint on the Window" in 2003,. Recently he has had poems published in *Madness Muse Press, Horror Sleaze Trash, the Rats's Ass Review, Roanoke Review, the Amethyst Review, Synchronized Chaos, Fixator Press, Beatnik Cowboy, Gargoyle, The Chamber Magazine* and *Blue Lake Review*.

Raymond Cummings resides in Owings Mills, Maryland. A 1999 graduate of Washington College, he is the author of books including *Assembling the Lord* and *From An Upstate Window*. His writing has appeared in *The Wire* magazine, *The Village Voice, Splice Today,* and the *Baltimore City Paper.*

Mel Edden is British poet whose recent work has been published in *The Loch Raven Review, Meat For Tea, Gargoyle Magazine* and *Welter*. She co-hosts Manor Mill's poetry events with Bob Bowie. She lives in Monkton with her husband and two delightfully rambunctious little Americans. Follow her on Instagram @ meledden for poetry updates.

Michael Fallon is the author of five published collections of poetry, *A History of the Color Black*, Dolphin-Moon Press, 1991; *Since You Have No Body*, winner of the Plan B Press Poetry Chapbook Competition, 2011; *The Great Before and After*, BrickHouse Books, 2011, and the self-published, *Empire of Leaves*, Singing Man Press, 2018. His recent poetry chapbook, *Leaf Notes: Poems of the Plague Years*, was published by Writer's Relief, and won the 2021 Water Sedge Poetry Prize.

Virginia Friedman is a mystic at heart and a Spiritual Care Director by profession. A graduate of Goucher College and Wesley Theological Seminary, she feels most alive when bringing comfort, hope, and joy to the sick and marginalized. She lives in Baltimore, enjoying time with family and friends, dancing, writing, being in nature, and pondering the sacred.

Jill Goodman. For Jill, writing has always been a steady companion. She is happiest with a flash of inspiration, notepad, and medium point pen. Professionally, she is a consultant for independent and private schools with over twenty years of experience working with organizational leaders to advance their school's mission and deliver on its promises. She wrote her first poems in 2023, encouraged by the Manor Mill writing community. Find her blog at jillgoodmanconsulting.com.

Clarinda Harriss, a professor emerita of English at Towson University, is the longtime publisher of BrickHouse Books, Inc., MD's oldest literary press. Her most recent poetry collections are *Innumerable Moons* and *Ash Wedding*.

Thom Hawkins is a writer and artist based in Maryland. He has written books soliciting anecdotes from people on a particular topic (*In Name Only, A First Time for Anything, Alphabetical Orders, Musical Madeleines*)—as well as children's books (*The Yeti Made Me Do It, Baldwin, Two Kings, Claudine*)—and has co-authored several poetry books (*Thirty Placebos; O, DeJoy; Slight Refreshments*). His video art and drawings have been displayed at exhibitions or in performances in Baltimore, Wilmington (DE), Philadelphia, and New York. Thom has also appeared with the Baltimore Improv Group, Ignite Baltimore, Ignite DC, and on The Stoop Storytelling podcast.

David Hofstetter is a retired administrative law judge who lives in Columbia with his wife and his dog, Watson. He enjoys chopping wood, cooking, doomscrolling, and pickleball.

Matt Hohner. An editor with *Loch Raven Review*, Matt Hohner (MFA, Naropa University) has published two collections: *At the Edge of a Thousand Years*, winner of the 2023 Jacar Press Poetry Book Contest, and *Thresholds and Other Poems* (Apprentice House 2018). He has held two residencies at the Virginia Center for the Creative Arts, with one forthcoming at Anam Cara in Ireland. His publications include *Rattle: Poets Respond, Takahē, New Contrast, Narrative Magazine, Poetry Ireland, Prairie Schooner, The Baltimore Review,* and elsewhere.

Stephen Hollaway left being a pastor after four decades to return to his first love, poetry. He recently completed an MFA in Creative Writing and Publishing Arts at the University of Baltimore. The poems in his first collection, *Tin Ear*, reflect his concerns as a seventy-year-old with aging—in particular the experience of hearing loss and tinnitus. Other poems deal with gun violence, mature faith, and his mother's depression. His work has appeared in *Passager* and *EcoTheo Review*. In May 2023 he won First Prize in Maryland Public Television's poetry contest and read the winning poem at Manor Mill.

John Hutchinson is a retired elementary school principal, married, and grandfather of thirteen. Various poetry collections written and published by John including *Beckoned by Water: Called to Other Shores* (2023) and *Abandon the Middle Way* (2012) are available for purchase on Amazon.com.

Jennifer Keith plays bass for the rock band Batworth Stone. Her poems have appeared in *Sewanee Theological Review, The Nebraska Review, The Free State Review, Fledgling Rag, Unsplendid, Best American Poetry 2015, JMWW,* and elsewhere. Keith received the 2014 John Elsberg poetry prize, and was a finalist in the 2021 Erskine J. Poetry Prize from Smartish Pace. Her first full-length book of poems, *Terminarch*, won the 2023 Able Muse Book Award and is due to publish in 2024. She lives in Baltimore, Maryland.

Ruhi Khanna has grown up in Baltimore County. She loves the hikes of Oregon Ridge and the mild four seasons in this area. Living with non-verbal autism, she has used many techniques to translate her thoughts to words and speech. The most successful has been to spell her thoughts on a letter board. Although this is exhausting for her and is not easy for everyone, we are thankful that she has found the way. She loves company and has enjoyed her evenings at Manor Mill listening to and reading poetry.

Zoe Leonard is a writer from Phoenix, Maryland. She is a Kundiman fellow and holds a BFA in Creative Writing from Emerson College. She is the social media manager for Manor Mill. You can connect with her on Instagram @zoe_leonard.storymode and read more work at zoe-leonard.com.

Steven Leyva was born in New Orleans, Louisiana and raised in Houston, Texas. His poems have appeared or are forthcoming in *2 Bridges Review, Scalawag, Nashville Review, jubilat, Vinyl, Prairie Schooner,* and *Best American Poetry 2020*. He is a Cave Canem fellow and author of the chapbook Low Parish and author of *The Understudy's Handbook* which won the Jean Feldman Poetry Prize from Washington Writers Publishing House. His second book of poems, *The Opposite of Cruelty*, is forthcoming from Blair Publishing in Spring 2025. Steven holds an MFA from the University of Baltimore, where he is an associate professor in the Klein Family School of Communications Design.

Kathy Mangan is the author of two full-length collections of poetry: *Above the Tree Line* (Carnegie Mellon U. Press) and *Taproot* (Passager Books). Her poems have been published in numerous journals and anthologies, including the *Southern Review, Shenandoah, the Gettysburg Review,* and the Pushcart Prize. She taught American Literature and Creative Writing for more than four decades at McDaniel College.

Kari Martindale is a Pushcart Prize-nominated poet and spoken word artist who has been published in a number of literary journals and anthologies. She sits on the Board of Maryland Writers' Association and is on the management team of EC Poetry & Prose. Kari has an M.A. in Linguistics, has visited all fifty States and over forty countries, and is a veteran of the US Air Force. She values kindness over niceness and justice over peace.

S.B. Merrow studied literature and Japanese, then apprenticed as a flute-maker. For years she worked with her hands and ears, crafting and restoring concert flutes for performers, collectors, and conservatories, before returning to her first love, poetry. Her chapbook, *Unpacking the China*, won QuillsEdge Press' 2016 competition. A full-length poetry collection, *Everyone A Bell*, was published in 2020 by Kelsay Books.

Derek Miller is a writer, musician, and Episcopal priest in the greater Baltimore area, working in a small church in the old mill town of Ellicott City. He and his family enjoy hiking, strolling on Main St, getting yummy beverages and treats, being with neighbors, exploring new places, and laughing a lot.

Erika Miller has family ties to St. James, Parkton and St. James Academy, Monkton. After retiring from teaching, she spends her time swimming, painting with watercolors and traveling. Poetry at Manor Mill is a new adventure which she is really enjoying.

Douglas Mowbray lives in Harford County, Maryland with his wife, Nayeli; and son, Emerson. His work has appeared in *The Baltimore Review, Welter, Urbanite, Linked Verse,* and *Found Poetry Review*. He has performed on stage for Mortified and the Interrobang Theatre Company in Baltimore, Maryland. Doug is a Board Member for BrickHouse Books; a former small press publisher (twentythreebooks); and co-founder of Poetry in Community and the Baltimore Poetry Library.

Matthew Milad Nikzad was born and raised in Perry Hall, Maryland, and is the son of Persian immigrants. Matt is currently working on his Master's in Genetic Counseling degree at the University of Maryland School of Medicine. He is also a classically-trained pianist and composer. He started writing poetry in high school and was encouraged to continue by his English teacher, Mrs. LeeAnne Richardson. She was also the one who introduced him to the vibrant and welcoming Manor Mill community.

Rachel M. Novak has worked for over two decades with a global organization and enjoys growing alongside her plants here in Maryland. An avid gardener and self-taught tea maker, other hobbies are writing, art, music and exploring nature. Rachel has attended Manor Mill's poetry open mic since the onset. She believes that a sense of wonder and a solid character are two important things you can instill at a young age, and must protect at all costs as time passes on.

Alan C. Reese is the author of the chapbook *Reports from Shadowland*. His work has appeared or is forthcoming in *Rain Taxi, Smartish Pace, Gargoyle, The Blue Mountain Review, The Baltimore Sun, Maryland Poetry Review, Potomac Review, Delaware Review, Welter, Grub Street, Attic, Bicycle Review, Danse Macabre,* and the *Loch Raven Review*. He was the editor and founder of *Dancing Shadow Review* and the president of Abecedarian Books, Inc., a small press publisher for ten years. He served as the president of the Harford Poetry Society for two years. He teaches writing at Towson University.

Gerhard "Gary" Siebert grew up in the '30s and '40s in Germany and came to the US in the mid '50s, served in the US Army between '57 and '63, had a successful career in Public Service, retired in early '90. After a loving marriage of nearly sixty years his wife departed for the Celestial Suburb in 2016. For twenty years Gary taught accounting as an adjunct professor at Johns Hopkins University. He is an avid sailor, a gourmand, loves and appreciates word games and keeps mentally and physically active. Presently he still resides in Towson, MD with his dog Skipper; living a mutedly happy bachelor's life.

Lauren H. Smith is a Baltimore poet, creative nonfiction writer, musician, floral designer, and pup mom. Her poetry and prose have been published in *Skelter, The Offbeat,* and *Hyssop + Laurel*. Lauren plays with imagery, rhythm, and inter-syllabic sounds while weaving in themes of beauty and grief, nostalgia and identity. Her words embody wonder and compassionate curiosity, as she believes these frameworks help us hope, heal, and become more fully who we are.

Heather Sowers lives with her cat Cleopatra just over the Maryland line and loves old time music and square dancing. An avid reader and writer, she believes in the healing power of the creative arts. As a social worker, she supports people in deepening connections to themselves, each other, the Earth and the Divine through embodied family, group and community experiences that are playfully therapeutic. Raised on a Midwest farm, she is passionate about nature and is thankful for sugar snap peas and lilacs.

Otis Sprow is from Baltimore and his work has been published in *The Ekphrastic Review* and his own self-published book, *Poems* (www.otisbook.com). He has also been a featured poet multiple times with the Short Story Book Fest and at multiple venues in the Baltimore area. He was the featured poet of record for the US Department of Housing and Urban Development 2022 Secretary's Award program.

David Stant's poetry focuses on his experience of adversity and his journey toward a better life. His work has appeared in the last four editions of *Maryland Bards Poetry Review* and he has had published two chapbooks, *Four Corners of Depression* and *Sounds of Silence* (2021 and 2024, J2B Publishing). David's poetry has also been selected for inclusion in *Train River Poetry Anthology Summer 2021* and *Bards Against Hunger Ten Year Anniversary Anthology*, two collections that include both nationally and internationally competitive writing. David resides on the border between Frederick City and surrounding country, and this convergence of cultures has inspired and shaped his writing.

Chrissy Stegman is a poet/writer from Baltimore, Maryland. Recent work has appeared or is forthcoming in: *Rejection Letters, Gone Lawn, Gargoyle Magazine, Anti-Heroin Chic, Poverty House, Stone Circle Review, Fictive Dream,* and *The Voidspace*. She is the winner of the 2022 Patricia Bibby Idyllwild scholarship for poetry and placed second for the 2022 HoCoPoLitSo Ellen Conroy Kennedy Poetry Prize. She is a 2023 Best of the Net nominee.

Jennifer A Sutherland is a poet and essayist in Baltimore, Maryland. She is the author of *Bullet Points: A Lyric* (River River Books, 2023). Her work has appeared or will soon appear in *Birmingham Poetry Review, Hopkins Review, Denver Quarterly, $ (Poetry is Currency), Cagibi* and elsewhere.

Nicole Tsygan has been writing poetry and reading at Manor Mill since she was seventeen. Nicole is currently attending college while pursuing a degree in Theatre. Someday, she hopes to get a degree in library science. Nicole has loved words all her life, spending time in plenty of libraries and on the stages of many a spelling bee. Oftentimes, you can find her listening to music, reading, and daydreaming snippets of poetry. Most of her poetry is written in the Notes app because, if there's one thing Nicole can't ever lose (and always has with her), it's her phone!

Kaitlin "Kait" Wachter has been writing poetry since her early teens. She likes to experiment with various styles and rhythms, and her topics range from whimsical humor to mental health. Ms. Wachter is currently a student at a local university. Aside from writing poems, she enjoys running, playing piano, reading research articles, and spending time with friends or her large Italian family.

Bolling Willse Sr. started thinking poetically in his teens as a young songwriter, moved by the times and artists like the Beatles and Otis Redding. Study of philosophy and American literature deepened his love of the written and spoken word. However, fatherhood, and a career in computing, channeled his creativity elsewhere. After losing his oldest son in a plane crash, and subsequently finding his journals, Bolling came to understand the healing value of words left behind by loved ones. Poetry at Manor Mill has helped him to rediscover his love of the written word and, more importantly, his love for reading aloud and telling stories that he found so rewarding as a father.

ACKNOWLEDGMENTS

All poems appear here with the permission of their author. Below we give credit to the publishers who offered these poems their first homes.

Robert R. Bowie Jr.'s "Predawn Swim" was originally published in *An Accidental Diary* (2021).

Shirley J. Brewer's "Modern Torso of Apollo" was originally published in *Slant* (Volume XXX, 2016) and *Wild Girls* (Apprentice House, 2023).

Dan Cuddy's "Traveling To Grafenwöhr During A Military Exercise" was originally published in *Pearl* (1988).

Michael Fallon's "A Poem for My Father" was originally published in *Weavings 2000: The Maryland Millennial Anthology* edited by Michael Glaser (Maryland Commission for Celebration 2000, St. Mary's City, MD. 2000: 181).

Matt Hohner's "Driving at Night in the Rain, April 2021" was originally published in *At the Edge of a Thousand Years* (Jacar Press, 2024).

Stephen Hollaway's "Losing My Hearing on Block Island" was originally published in *Tin Ear* (Gray Noise, Baltimore, 2023).

John Hutchinson's "God's Work" was originally published in *Abandon the Middle Way* (Kindle Direct Publishing, 2023).

Jennifer Keith's "Rom Com" won second place in the 2024 Eastern Shore Writers Association Crossroads poetry contest was published in their 2024 *Bay to Ocean Journal*.

Steven Leyva's "The Inner Harbor's Octave" was originally published in *The Understudy's Handbook* (Washington Writers' Publishing House, 2020).

Kathy Mangan's "Husking Corn for Dinner, She Thinks of an Old Boyfriend" was originally published in *Taproot* (Passager, 2019).

S. B. Merrow's "Genesis" was originally published in *Everyone A Bell* (Kelsay Books, 2020).

Alan C. Reese's "In the Valley of Echoes" was originally published in *Smartish Pace* (Issue 20, April 2013). It was a Finalist in the 12th Annual Erskine J. Poetry Prize.

David Stant's "In Memory" was originally published in *Sounds of Silence* (J2B Publishing, 2024)

Chrissy Stegman's "A Pilgrim's Pace" was originally published in *Blue Heron Review* (Issue 16, Spring 2023)

Jennifer A Sutherland's "Positioning" was originally published in *I-70 Review* (Fall 2020) and was selected by Kaveh Akbar for inclusion in Best New Poets 2021.

www.ingramcontent.com/pod-product-compliance
Lightning Source LLC
Chambersburg PA
CBHW050817090426
42736CB00022B/3489